MEDIA OWNERSHIP

Essential Viewpoints

MEDIA
OWNERSHIP
BY TOM ROBINSON

Content Consultant
Mary McIlrath, PhD
Market Research Consultant

ABDO
Publishing Company

CREDITS

Published by ABDO Publishing Company, 8000 West 78th Street, Edina, Minnesota 55439. Copyright © 2010 by Abdo Consulting Group, Inc. International copyrights reserved in all countries. No part of this book may be reproduced in any form without written permission from the publisher. The Essential Library™ is a trademark and logo of ABDO Publishing Company.

Printed in the United States.

Editor: Erika Wittekind
Copy Editor: Paula Lewis
Interior Design and Production: Emily Love
Cover Design: Emily Love

Library of Congress Cataloging-in-Publication Data
Robinson, Tom, 1964–
  Media ownership / By Tom Robinson.
    p. cm. — (Essential viewpoints)
  Includes bibliographical references and index.
  ISBN 978-1-60453-534-1
  1. Broadcasting—Law and legislation—United States—Juvenile literature. 2. Mass media—Law and legislation—United States—Juvenile literature. I. Title.
  KF2805.Z9R62 2009
  343.7309'9—dc22
                                    2008034909

Media Ownership

TABLE OF CONTENTS

FCC Chairman Kevin Martin speaks at a hearing regarding cross-ownership limits on December 18, 2007, at the FCC headquarters.

MEDIA CONSOLIDATION

*I*n 1975, the Federal Communications Commission (FCC) created the newspaper/broadcast cross-ownership ban. Under this ban, the joint ownerships of newspapers and television or radio stations in the same market were prohibited, except for those in place prior to 1975.

But should the government limit how many media outlets one person or company owns? What should those limitations be? These questions had been a subject of debate long before 1975. And they would continue to be the subject of debate.

By 1996, the FCC had acknowledged the need to consider change. In 2003, it began making adjustments to rules while encouraging public discussion on the issues. In 2007, the FCC voted to reduce restrictions on cross-ownership in some of the nation's largest markets. This rule would allow newspapers in any of the nation's top 20 media markets to also own a television or radio station in the same market.

But in May 2008, the Senate challenged the FCC's proposed rule and voted against it and the idea of consolidating the media. The Senate urged the House to do the same, even though President George W. Bush had indicated he was prepared to veto the bill.

THE HEART OF THE CONTROVERSY

Opponents and proponents of media deregulation disagree over whether a free-market economy or more government control would better serve the public interest. Deregulation can lead to the creation of fewer, larger media companies controlling the flow of information. But others argue that the alternative is government interference in an industry that often best serves society by being a watchdog of government actions.

Major Markets

According to Nielsen Media Research, the top 20 television markets in the United States are:
1. New York
2. Los Angeles
3. Chicago
4. Philadelphia
5. Dallas-Fort Worth
6. San Francisco-Oakland-San Jose
7. Boston
8. Atlanta
9. Washington DC
10. Houston
11. Detroit
12. Phoenix
13. Tampa-St. Petersburg
14. Seattle-Tacoma
15. Minneapolis-St. Paul
16. Miami-Fort Lauderdale
17. Cleveland-Akron
18. Denver
19. Orlando-Daytona Beach
20. Sacramento

Ownership of media outlets by too few companies creates the possibility that Americans will receive their news from limited sources. Such narrow coverage might not represent the views and needs of society as a whole. Restricting ownership combinations, however, also has its downside. Regulations might make it difficult or impossible for some newspapers and news stations to be successful in a time when the media business is changing. If media outlets need to cut jobs or to go out of business, that also could decrease the amount of news and viewpoints that are available to the public.

The FCC's rule change addressed the largest media markets first, in part because those markets already included many options. With additional stations in each large market, the chances were less that two companies with shared ownership would significantly reduce the presence of diverse opinions. The ruling assured that a certain number of stations in each market would remain independent.

FCC Chairman Kevin Martin said the issue was the most controversial to ever be addressed by the commission. Martin said the move helped newspaper companies that had been hurt by reductions in circulation and advertising revenues. The FCC wanted to preserve as much diversity of opinion while keeping media companies competitive in a changing marketplace.

Critics, however, questioned that the relaxation of restrictions could be the beginning of a trend of change that threatened the way Americans received news and commentary. *Seattle Times* publisher Frank Blethen said continued consolidation of media ownership was a threat to democracy.

History

The FCC created the cross-ownership ban in 1975. It prohibits a newspaper and a television or radio station in the same market from being owned by the same company. Newspaper/broadcast ownership combinations already in place were allowed to remain.

Beginning in 2003, the FCC began limiting some ownership in certain situations rather than banning it altogether. Three years later, the FCC sought public comment on how it should address newspaper/broadcast cross-ownership issues. The comment phase included public hearings that helped shape the decisions made in 2007.

DIFFERENCE OF OPINION

The Telecommunications Act of 1996 required the FCC to periodically review its broadcast ownership rules to determine whether the rules continued to serve the public interest in terms of competition. After reviewing its rules in 2002, the FCC proposed making changes. It created new cross-media ownership limits and revised the rules on ownership of multiple local television stations. It also changed the way it counted radio stations within a market for purposes of determining limits.

On June 2, 2003, the FCC voted 3-2 to make the changes and recommend that Congress lift the cross-ownership ban. Opponents immediately expressed concern. Terence Smith of the Public Broadcasting Service summarized the concerns during a report on the *NewsHour with Jim Lehrer*:

Specifically, the new rules state that in the largest cities, one company may own up to three television stations. Nationally, a company can own stations that reach 45 percent of U.S. households, up from 35 percent. One company can own a broadcast outlet and a newspaper in the same city, ending the rule against cross-ownership in all but the smallest markets. The outnumbered Democrats on the

Newspapers in Decline

In 2008, Kevin J. Martin was chairman of the FCC. He used the situation of newspapers to help explain the FCC's decision to relax limits on newspaper/broadcast station cross-ownership. Martin contributed to the *New York Times* opinion page on November 13, 2007. According to Martin, the financial struggles of newspapers played into the decision:

In many towns and cities, the newspaper is an endangered species. At least 300 daily papers have stopped publishing in the last 30 years. Those newspapers that have survived are struggling financially. Newspaper circulation has declined steadily for more than 10 years. . . . If we don't act to improve the health of the newspaper industry, we will see newspapers wither and die. Without newspapers, we would be less informed about our communities and have fewer outlets for the expression of independent thinking and a diversity of viewpoints. The challenge is to restore the viability of newspapers while preserving the core values of a diversity of voices and a commitment to localism in the media marketplace.[1]

commission argued that the new rules mean a single company could conceivably own up to three television stations, eight radio stations, the cable television system and cable TV stations, and the only daily newspaper in a single city.[2]

The debate turned into a political issue split along party lines, even within the FCC. Republicans backed the changes, citing the benefits of consolidation. Republican Commissioner Kathleen Abernathy said that the prospect of a media monopoly was a myth. "It is simply not possible to monopolize the flow of information in today's world," she said. "Indeed, the fall of communism in the 1980s and the end of military dictatorships in the 1990s shows that diverse viewpoints cannot be suppressed even by authoritarian governments much less by private companies."[3]

Democrats fought back, saying the changes went against the country's best interests. Michael J. Copps, the senior Democrat on the FCC, was one who held this view. "This path surrenders to a handful of corporations awesome powers over our news, information, and entertainment," Copps said. "On this path, we endanger time-honored safeguards and time-proven values that have strengthened the country, as well as the media."[4]

David Hughey, publisher of the Herald-Sun, tells newsroom employees of the newspaper's transfer of ownership in 2005.

The criticism led to *Prometheus v. FCC*, a court case brought before the Third Circuit Court of Appeals. The court was expected either to agree with the FCC's actions and uphold them, or disagree with the decisions and overturn them. Instead of accepting either side of the controversy, the Third Circuit chose a third option. The court affirmed some of the decisions of the FCC. And without overturning others, the court held the commission accountable for either justifying or modifying some of the proposals.

THE DEBATE CONTINUES

Researchers have sought to determine whether cross-ownership between newspapers and television stations really does have an impact on coverage. A 2003 study by the Project for Excellence in Journalism looked at markets that had grandfathered cross-ownership of newspaper and broadcast stations in place. It determined that "stations with cross-ownership—in which the parent company also owns a newspaper in the same market—tended to produce higher quality newscasts."[5] The same study did not address how the cross-ownership affected newspaper coverage.

Jeffrey Milyo is a professor of economics and public affairs at the University of Missouri. He conducted a 2007 study titled "The Effects of Cross-ownership on the Local Content and Political Slant of Local Television News." Milyo received some assistance from the FCC in

Cross-ownership in Major Markets

Prior to a 2008 agreement to sell controlling interest in *Newsday* to Cablevision, the Tribune Company had cross-ownership in the nation's three largest media markets. This cross-ownership was grandfathered in along with the FCC rules in 1975. The Tribune Company owned *Newsday* and television station WPIX in New York, the *Los Angeles Times* and television station KTLA in Los Angeles, and the *Chicago Tribune* and superstation WGN in Chicago. The only other cross-ownership existing in any of the top five markets at the time was between the *New York Post* and television stations WWOR and WYNY in New York.

gathering data for his study. Milyo also noted the positive effects of cross-ownership:

> This analysis reveals that local television newscasts for cross-owned stations contain on average about one [to] two minutes more news coverage overall, or 4 percent [to] 8 percent more than the average for non-cross-owned stations. Newspaper cross-ownership is also significantly and positively associated with both local news coverage and local political news coverage. Cross-owned stations show 7 percent [to] 10 percent more local news than do non-cross-owned stations (regardless of whether sports and weather segments are included in this comparison); further, on average, cross-owned stations broadcast about 25 percent more coverage of state and local politics. Newspaper ownership is also associated with more candidate coverage, more candidate speaking time, and more coverage of opinion polls.[6]

The FCC made a similar argument when making its case to the Third Circuit Court in 2004. The Court disagreed, however, with the specific limits the FCC was choosing for future cross-ownership decisions. The Third Circuit's decision withstood an appeal to the Supreme Court in 2005. The FCC's interpretation of research and the Third Circuit ruling were not enough to end the controversy.

The Senate followed through with plans to oppose the FCC's revisions on cross-ownership rules in 2008.

Senator Byron Dorgan, a Democrat from North Dakota, introduced a bill that threw out the new FCC rules. Cosponsors of the bill included Hillary Clinton from New York and Barack Obama from Illinois. Dorgan said the FCC rules would open loopholes that would allow more newspaper and television station mergers across the country. "We already have too much concentration in the media," Dorgan said. "Diverse, independent, and local media sources are essential to ensuring that the public has access to a variety of information."[7]

Following the Senate's decision, Copps again spoke out against the decision his commission made. Copps had been in the minority on the vote. "The Senate spoke for a huge majority of Americans last night by voting to overturn the flawed FCC decision gutting our long-standing ban on newspaper-broadcast cross-ownership. With courageous leaders like Senator Byron Dorgan, the Senate has struck a blow for localism and diversity in a media environment crying out for more of both."[8]

A protester wears a cardboard television cutout at a 2003 public hearing on proposed changes to media ownership rules.

The Titanic *departs England in 1912. Problems sending distress signals when the ship sank led to some early attempts at regulating the airwaves.*

Communications Law

The U.S. government first became involved in legislating broadcast communications early in the twentieth century. The Wireless Ship Act was passed on June 24, 1910, and became effective on July 1, 1911. The act required some ships to have a skilled radio operator and equipment capable of transmitting a message 100 miles (160 km). It applied to all ocean passenger vessels carrying 50 or more people from U.S. ports to locations 200 miles (320 km) or more away.

Within months, Congress worked on adjusting the bill so that all ships with 50 or more passengers would be required to have two radio operators. This would allow for breaks and sleep time for the operators. Congress saw the need for more changes following the sinking of the *Titanic* in 1912. The ships traveling closest to the tragedy did not pick up distress signals sent by the *Titanic*.

The Radio Act of 1912 allowed Congress to take control of radio frequencies in general. Congress gave the secretary of commerce and labor the authority to issue licenses and frequencies to radio stations and to U.S. citizens. The act provided some order and made boat travel safer. Still, it did not give the secretary of commerce and labor the power to reject license requests. As the number of companies and individuals transmitting radio signals continued to grow, more legislation followed. With safety addressed, the government had other issues to handle.

Public Interest

Congress was faced with balancing issues of free speech against the concepts of public interest in the buildup to passing the Radio Act of 1927. One of its goals was to restrict clutter across the airwaves. It also managed who received licenses for the limited range of available frequencies.

By 1926, thousands of stations held licenses. The U.S. Department of Commerce had hundreds more applications to process and no

The *Titanic* Changed History

A disaster at sea led Congress to realize a need to protect not only those aboard ships, but throughout the country as well. When the *Titanic* sank, faulty radio communications played a role in pushing the death total to approximately 1,500.

The *Titanic* was a luxury passenger ship traveling from Southampton, England, to New York City. It struck an iceberg hundreds of miles off the coast of Newfoundland, Canada. Historian Susan Douglas, author of *Inventing American Broadcasting, 1899–1922*, researched the use of radio by the *Titanic*. According to Douglas, two ships that were half a day's travel away successfully picked up the distress message. The message was also picked up by the passenger steamship *Carpathia*, which was 58 miles (93 km) away. Two closer ships missed the call—one because it lacked equipment, and the other because its lone radio operator was asleep.

The *Titanic* was under icy water in less than three hours. The *Carpathia* arrived three and a half hours after receiving the message. It could only help those who had made it into lifeboats. According to Douglas, the Wireless Ship Act of 1910 was not strong enough to save the majority of the passengers. She pointed out that radios were not manned—or even turned on—24 hours per day. "There were loopholes in the law," Douglas wrote.[1]

authority to reject any of them. The result was that station signals overlapped and interfered with each other. The number of users threatened the quality of radio in general. The Congress questioned what this would mean for the future of the airwaves.

The Radio Act of 1927 created the Federal Radio Commission (FRC), the forerunner to the Federal Communications Commission (FCC). The FRC was created to regulate the industry in a way that best served the public interest. President Calvin Coolidge signed the Radio Act of 1927 into law on February 23, 1927.

The FRC created a policy statement in 1928 to clarify its intentions. It stated that broadcasters should not use the airwaves to promote their own interests. Rather, stations should be used for purposes that best serve the audience. The FRC received more applications than the number of channels available. Therefore, it had to use discretion to determine which broadcasters would use those channels to best serve the public interest.

The Sherman Antitrust Act

The Sherman Antitrust Act, passed in 1890, was designed to fight monopolies and limit other actions that restrained free trade and economic competition. The act, which was named after Senator John Sherman of Ohio, was the first federal action of its kind. Several states already had similar laws. The Federal Trade Commission was created in 1914 by the Federal Trade Commission Act. Its purpose is to protect consumers and eliminate unfair labor practices.

POLITICAL CONCERNS

The Federal Radio Commission had clear
political concerns when deciding which broadcasts
should receive licenses. Senator Key Pittman
of Nevada and Representative E. L. Davis of
Tennessee were proponents of controlling potential
monopolies. They saw the Radio Corporation of
America as a potential monopolistic force in the
early evolution of the radio industry.

In 1927, while recognizing the need to protect
free speech, Congress also was concerned with
protecting the public from indecency. The Radio
Act included this declaration: "No person within
the jurisdiction of the United States shall utter any
obscene, indecent, or profane language by means
of radio communication."[2] Congress members
recognized radio's extensive exposure to citizens.
This included public places where individuals do
not necessarily choose the station to which they
are listening. Congress perceived an obligation to
protect people from profane language and indecent
messages.

Members of the public weighed in through
letters to members of Congress. Their main
concern was about eliminating radio interference

Pittsburgh radio station KDKA broadcasts in 1920. KDKA was credited with the first radio news report.

to receive a clearer signal. Fewer people wrote to the congressmen with free speech concerns.

The Radio Act was written in a way to protect a balance of political expression between Republicans and Democrats. Concerns of the times, in regards to communism and socialism, led to limitations on access to candidates from other political parties.

Laws Evolve

The Communications Act of 1934 combined some previously existing rules and laws. It also created the FCC, replacing the FRC. The new

"We hear a great deal about the freedom of the air, but there are two parties to freedom of the air, and to freedom of speech for that matter. There is the speechmaker and the listener. Certainly in radio I believe in freedom for the listener."[3]

—*Secretary of Commerce Herbert Hoover, 1925*

commission had additional responsibilities.

Prior to the Communications Act of 1934, telegraph and telephone services were under the authority of the post office and the Interstate Commerce Commission. President Franklin D. Roosevelt wanted to change this. He believed that all electronic communications should be regulated by a single agency. On February 26, 1934, Roosevelt formally urged Congress to take such action. The laws were finalized by June 9 and took effect in July.

The FCC has remained in place since 1934, but laws involving communications continue to be the subject of debate. Television, radio, newspaper, and the Internet all relate to each other, and each continues to evolve.

New communications acts were passed in 1966 and 1996. Debate on media-related issues has intensified since 1996. Controversial discussions continue on how to interpret existing laws and on which laws still need further adjustment to match a changing world. ⌐

Members of the FCC appear at a Senate subcommittee hearing
on communications in 1961.

The building housing the Federal Communications Commission shown in 1969. The headquarters has now expanded to a larger building nearby.

THE FEDERAL
COMMUNICATIONS
COMMISSION

he Federal Communications Commission (FCC) and the media have had a complex relationship for approximately three-quarters of a century. The FCC was created to oversee telecommunications. Media outlets use telecommunications to distribute information throughout the United States.

The media has undergone drastic change since the FCC was formed in 1934. Much of this is due to developing technology. In turn, the FCC also has changed. According to FCC Chairman Kevin J. Martin, the FCC had to ease up on cross-ownership restrictions to protect an important industry. He argued that media outlets needed more flexibility to cope with their economic circumstances as new competitors emerged.

Some critics believe that the FCC has strayed from its original mission. FCC critics say the agency is allowing itself to be influenced by the very organizations it is intended to control. Even with the FCC, the potential for influence by big media companies has grown. These companies play a large role in driving public opinion and affecting politics.

The Early Days

The FCC began operation on July 11, 1934, just a month after it was created by the Communications Act of 1934. The act includes a description of its mission:

The Chairmen

Some facts about the FCC's chairmen:

• Fourteen Democrats, including the first seven to hold the position, and twelve Republicans have served as chairmen.

• Rosel Hyde was the first Republican chairman and was also one of two to hold the position twice. Hyde was chairman from 1953 to 1954 and again from 1966 to 1969. Paul Walker was chairman in 1947 and again from 1952 to 1953.

• Four chairmen were appointed and resigned in the same year: Ewell Jett (1944), Paul Walker, Robert E. Lee (1981), and James Quello (1993).

• The average stay in the position is less than three years.

• Mark Fowler held the position the longest (1981 to 1987).

For the purpose of regulating interstate and foreign commerce in communication by wire and radio so as to make available, so far as possible, to all the people of the United States . . . a rapid, efficient, nationwide, and worldwide wire and radio communication service with adequate facilities at reasonable charges.[1]

The FCC was also responsible for ensuring that wire and radio communication would be used to promote safety of life and of property.

The Communications Act of 1934 stated that no more than four commissioners could be from the same political party. An amendment to the act in July 1983 reduced the number of commissioners from seven to five. The maximum representing one party was decreased from four to three.

Members of the first FCC are pictured on July 11, 1934.

The FCC's current directive is to regulate interstate and international communication by radio, television, wire, satellite, and cable. The commissioners are responsible for supervising and delegating responsibilities to staff, bureaus, and committees.

Higher Profile

Through the years, the FCC commissioners and chairmen often would not be recognized outside media and political circles. That changed in 2001 when President George W. Bush appointed Michael Powell as chairman. Powell, 37, was a military veteran and the son of Secretary of State Colin Powell.

With strong support from Bush, Michael Powell went against many of the trends that had been created throughout the FCC's history. Some thought Powell was necessarily reacting to changes in the marketplace. Others criticized him for catering to the interests of big businesses that supported Bush.

In a 2001 speech before the Federal Communications Bar Association, Powell explained his views. He thought the media should be treated

---

FCC Structure

The Federal Communications Commission is directed by five commissioners. Each is appointed by the president and confirmed by the Senate for five-year terms, except when filling an unexpired term. The president designates one commissioner as chairperson. None of the commissioners are allowed to have a financial interest in any commission-related business.

The commission staff operates seven bureaus and ten staff offices:

- Bureaus: Consumer and Governmental Affairs, Enforcement, International, Media, Wireless Telecommunications, Public Safety and Homeland Security, Wireline Competition
- Offices: Administrative Law Judges, Communications Business Opportunities, Engineering and Technology, General Counsel, Inspector General, Legislative Affairs, Managing Director, Media Relations, Strategic Planning and Policy Analysis, Workplace Diversity

using traditional U.S. business practices based on
a free market. He said the promarket tradition had
created better products and services for citizens.
Such a market, in his view, let consumers choose
products and encouraged entrepreneurs to find new
ideas to provide those choices. Supply and demand
help set prices, and consumers benefit from efficient
businesses.

Powell made no secret that he saw a need for
change in the way the FCC set policy. In Powell's
view, if a rule was not clearly and specifically
relevant, the FCC should get rid of it. In his opening
remarks after being appointed, Powell said that
deregulation means to "validate the purpose of a rule
in the modern context, or eliminate it. As simple as
that."[2]

Senator Fritz Hollings, a Democrat from South
Carolina, strongly disagreed. "That, my friends,
is not the law," Hollings said during a hearing on
media consolidation later that year.[3]

Powell was undeterred. Days later, he granted
a waiver to Rupert Murdoch's News Corporation,
allowing it to obtain ten more television stations.
Without the waiver, one of Bush's most influential
supporters would have been unable to make the

acquisition. News Corporation would have been in violation of the cross-ownership ban and national ownership limits. Commissioner Gloria Tristiani, who voted against the merger, wrote that the 3–2 decision "shows the length the Commission will go to avoid standing in the way of media mergers."[4]

Small radio stations were acquired by big media companies in large numbers. In the process, ownership by minorities and by women dropped to well below 4 percent by 2005. "I don't think anybody anticipated that the pace would be so fast and so dramatic," said William Kennard, who was Powell's predecessor. "The fundamental economic structure of the radio industry is changing from one of independently owned operators to something akin to a chain store."[5] As with chain stores, the networks of stations were in a position to operate more efficiently, according to Kennard.

Former FCC Chairman Michael Powell speaks at a news conference in 2003.

Newspapers from different publishers are displayed for sale in Canberra, Australia. The country heavily regulates media ownership.

OTHER COUNTRIES

Other countries also have dealt with the question of how to regulate telecommunications. In 1968, Canada's Parliament established the Canadian Radio-television and Telecommunications Commission (CRTC). The agency is similar to the United States' Federal

Communications Commission (FCC). Much like its U.S. equivalent, the CRTC has gone through many changes over the years.

The independent public authority's role was defined in 1985 under the Canadian Radio-television and Telecommunications Commission Act. Subsequent legislation helped clarify how the CRTC regulates the Canadian broadcasting system and telecommunications system. The CRTC reports to Parliament through the Minister of Canadian Heritage.

Similar Issues

Cross-ownership issues were at the forefront of CRTC's new policies announced on January 15, 2008. It said these new rules would maintain diversity among the voices heard through the Canadian broadcasting system.

When it made the revisions, the CRTC was satisfied with the current service and wide range of views being produced by the Canadian media. It kept policies that limited the number of television and radio stations that one person could control in the same market. It also created cross-media rules that limit control of different types of media—a local radio station, a local television station, or a local newspaper—to two in the same market.

CRTC Chairman Konrad von Finckenstein explained the benefits of the new policies in a press release. He said they would set a clear way for handling decisions regarding broadcasters in the future. Moreover, it would help maintain a diversity of voices being heard in the media and the variety of programming available, according to Finckenstein.

The CRTC's press release explained the organization's position. As more media companies consolidated, concern increased about the possibility that most coverage would be provided by a small number of large entities. Audiences would then suffer from a lack of diversity in content at the local, regional, and national levels. This prompted the CRTC to limit the issuance of broadcasting licenses to prevent one party from owning more than 45 percent of a market.

The CRTC pledged that it would quickly approve licenses that would

Journalistic Independence Code

The Canadian Broadcast Standards Council created a Journalistic Independence Code in January 2008. The council set minimum numbers of journalists to serve on its panels that study complaints. The code is intended to ensure diversity of professional editorial voices while monitoring broadcasters who own a newspaper in the same market. The use of journalists is intended to provide experts who fully understand the workings of a newsroom when assessing complaints.

Standard Broadcasting President Gary Slaight, left, and Astral Media President Ian Greenberg announce the Canadian companies' merger.

result in a party controlling less than 35 percent of the market share. But it would carefully examine transactions that would result in control between 35 and 45 percent. After a license was approved, an ownership group would be free to grow their existing assets to beyond 45 percent of an audience share through development of their product.

For the most part, the CRTC does not have jurisdiction over newspapers and Internet media. The exception is cases where cross-ownership issues are involved between newspapers and broadcast outlets.

AROUND THE WORLD

Prior to its changes in 2008, the CRTC sought to make educated decisions based on the evolving media world. "Media mergers and acquisitions have become common place over the last two decades, not only involving companies in the United States, but also companies around the globe," professors Alan Albarran and Bozena Mierzejewska wrote in a presentation at the Sixth World Media Economic Conference in Montreal in 2004.[1]

Michael McEwen was commissioned by the CRTC in May 2007 to provide a report on media ownership issues and how other countries deal with them around the globe. McEwen quoted Albarran and Mierzejewska's work while summing up his assignment in his report to the CRTC:

> The mergers and acquisitions continue both with the giants like the GE-owned NBC Universal but also in national circumstances including our own national market in Canada. Broadcasting and distribution are not the only media affected; newspapers and publishing continue to be part of cross media conglomerate growth. This is all happening within the existing rules and regulations of national and international market places.

Many analysts and observers equate media pluralism with a diversity of ownership and that concentration of ownership will skew public discussion by not exploring all viewpoints and interests. In their view, this can lead to abuse in political and policy decision making. [2]

McEwen found that policies and regulations generally had existed in individual sectors of television, radio, and print along with rules that applied across multiple industries. A few laws concerning "new media," meaning the Internet and other evolving technologies, had been added in recent years. Technology was creating new markets and opportunities, but new issues and legal challenges also needed to be addressed.

The media industry was going through changes that coincided with the intensifying of the old political debate of free-market economy versus government control. Too little government input left open the risk of monopolies. This could ultimately reduce the flow of information. Others think that governments should not have a hand in determining who provides what information.

Country by Country

The CRTC studied how many countries regulated media issues. McEwen's research provided much of the background, including statistical data.

Australia updated its Broadcasting Service Act of 1992 in April 2007. Australia's laws limit one person from controlling more than one broadcast license in one area or in combined areas that cover more than 75 percent of the population. The country also limits foreign ownership. Limits are placed on combined foreign ownership in national and metropolitan newspapers at 30 percent and single foreign ownership at 25 percent. The combined limit on foreign ownership of provincial and suburban newspapers is 50 percent of the population.

The amendments of 2007 loosened some of Australia's rules. Still, the country is regarded as heavily regulated. There is a two-out-of-three rule in terms of cross-ownership. This means that a person can control media operations in one market in two out of three among radio, television, and newspapers, but not all three.

In France, an owner may not be involved on the national level in more than two of the following:

❖ television audience area of more than 4 million people;

❖ radio audience area of more than 30 million people;

❖ cable audience area of more than 6 million people;

❖ or more than 20 percent of the national circulation of daily newspapers.

Similar restrictions, based on different numbers, are placed on local ownership within an area. Under these media rules, the French radio industry has grown to include approximately 1,200 stations.

Much of the media regulation in Germany is handled on the state level. One company's media holdings, including newspapers, are not supposed to exceed a 30 percent share in the market. The limit is 25 percent for media holdings strictly in television. Otherwise, cross-ownership is legal. This system appears to have worked for Germany. A diverse print media features 138 different publishers of Germany's 359 daily newspapers. By comparison, there were 290 owners of the 1,437 daily newspapers in the United States in 2006.

Private television and radio station ownership
occurred in Austria for the first time in 1997. The
first private television network began in 2003.
One entity is not allowed to own more than one
radio or television license in a given area. However,
one company often controls the dominant radio,
television, and newspaper outlets in a given market.

New Zealand has no limits on cross-ownership
or foreign ownership. In 1980, New Zealand
deregulated all of its communications, along with
much of its industry and economy. The small
country, with a population of just 4 million, receives
almost all of its television from foreign ownership
and programming.

The United Kingdom set up the Office of
Communications in 2003 to oversee media
ownership. The office looks at media mergers in
three different ways to make sure they meet public-
interest standards. First, at least three separate media
companies have to provide radio, television, and
newspaper service in each area. Anyone controlling
more than 20 percent of national newspaper
circulation cannot own more than 20 percent of an
independent television license. Anyone who owns
an independent television license cannot control

more than 20 percent of the newspaper market in that region or a radio station with more than 45 percent coverage in that same area.

POWERFUL FIGURES

Rupert Murdoch, through his News Corporation, is not only powerful in the United States. His media operation controls much of the industry in his native country of Australia as well as in the United Kingdom. Australia's limited diversity of media ownership and rules that limit foreigners from the market have contributed to News Corporation and John Fairfax Holdings dominating much

Limited Diversity in Austria

Josef Trappel, a professor at is the University of Zurich in Switzerland, is an expert on European media. He wrote about the media situation in Austria. Although an Austrian court has determined that the approved mergers do not harm media diversity, Trappel thinks that cross-ownership of different media outlets by the same companies has taken its toll in the country:

Another strand of controversial media policy concerns the unprecedented high degree of media ownership concentration in Austria. The largest newspaper equally owns the terrestrial national radio channel, and in almost all provinces the dominant newspaper publisher also owns the main radio channel and in some cases also the regional television channel. This concentration happened despite the fact that the cartel law in Austria requires the Cartel Court to check whether the merger or acquisition in question would endanger journalistic and media diversity.[3]

of the Australian media. Murdoch, who was born in Australia, overcame the obstacle of foreign ownership limits in the U.S. media when he became a U.S. citizen in 1985.

Murdoch has had a favorable relationship with powerful government leaders. He has been perceived to have close ties to President George W. Bush and the late President Ronald Reagan. That type of influence is one thing for a powerful media broker. Italy's Silvio Berlusconi tried to use even more influence.

Berlusconi was not only prime minister of Italy but also one of the nation's most powerful media personalities. Berlusconi, owner of the world-famous soccer club A.C. Milan, controlled the nation's three largest private television stations and its largest magazine. Some people questioned whether his ability to control media messages in Italy had contributed to his power.

Rupert Murdoch controls much of the media in his native Australia and in the United Kingdom.

One of the main concerns in the media-ownership debate is the availability of diverse and local news sources.

DIVERSIFICATION

Multiple organizations working together in a cooperative mode or under joint ownership can reduce costs. This helps keep media outlets viable in a time when they are facing potential financial crises. Safeguarding a troubled industry, particularly in the case of newspapers, has been a priority for many. This goal is the most common explanation for changes that have made it easier for media companies to merge and larger companies to buy up smaller companies. The Internet era has contributed to reduced newspaper circulation figures. Newspapers also have experienced a reduction in classified ad revenues for job listings and similar items that are now more commonly found online.

Federal Communications Commission (FCC) Chairman Kevin Martin said the rule restricting cross-ownership has been the only policy regarding ownership to remain unchanged since the 1970s. He said that FCC chairmen in the last decade, regardless of political affiliation, have considered changes necessary. Martin explained why in a 2007 *New York Times* editorial:

> *The ban on newspapers owning a broadcast station in their local markets may end up hurting the quality of news and the commitment of news organizations to their local communities. Newspapers in financial difficulty often have little choice but to scale back news gathering to cut costs. Allowing cross-ownership may help to forestall the erosion in local news*

coverage by enabling companies that own both newspapers and broadcast stations to share some costs.[1]

Public Interests

The concentration of media ownership already has been shifting as big media operations buy up smaller television and radio stations. At the same time, several advocacy groups have taken up the cause, trying to slow the rush to change cross-ownership rules.

Author Eric Klinenberg traveled the country gathering research for his 2007 book, *Fighting for Air: The Battle to Control America's Media.* He gathered examples of Americans who were not convinced that Martin's perception was accurate. Klinenberg talked about the experience in an interview. He argued that media consolidation would not serve the public's interests. Historically, diversity of ownership and local coverage have served the public best, Klinenberg said. In his travels, Klinenberg says he found many who agreed with this position:

> *This is an area that I think is kind of a no-brainer for most Americans. If you ask anyone, "Do you want someone like Rupert Murdoch to be able to come in and control your*

newspaper, three of your television stations, eight of your radio stations?" I think it's pretty clear that that's something that does not serve democracy well.[2]

BROADCAST RESULTS

Beyond the newspaper industry, diversity of voice can be affected through the increased consolidation of the radio and television industry. Diversity issues extend beyond the news and news commentary portion of the media. Entertainment is affected as well, with chains of radio stations creating formats that repeat the same content around the country. Some say these practices allow cost-effective ways of presenting the most popular music and programming to the most people. Others argue that they often ignore regional interests and avoid the risks of testing new genres.

New York Times columnist William Safire mourned the loss of variety on the airwaves in a column he wrote in 2003. He pointed out that in 1996, the top two broadcasting companies

Raising the Bar

Television-station ownership limits increased from 7 to 12 stations in 1984, as long as those stations did not exceed 25 percent of the national audience. In 1996, the limit increased to 35 percent of the national audience. The number was increased again in 2004 to 39 percent.

owned just over a hundred stations. When he wrote the column in 2003, that number had grown to more than 1,400. Previously, a "handful of owners" accounted for 20 percent of all industry revenue. In 2003, they raked in 55 percent of profits in local radio. "Take a listen to what's happened to local radio in one short wave of deregulation," Safire wrote. "The great cacophony of different sounds and voices is being amalgamated and homogenized. . . . Yesterday's programming diversity on the public's airwaves has degenerated to the Top 40."[3]

Others believe that while diversity may have value, it is not the government's place to ensure diversity through regulation. Adam Thierer is a senior fellow with the Progress & Freedom Foundation, a free-market-oriented think tank. Thierer sees government intervention as unnecessary. "We are living in a golden age of media, with more choices than ever," he said. "If

Delivering Diversity

More owners does not always mean more diverse content, points out *Slate* magazine editor Jack Shafer: "Wherever a broadcaster consolidates ownership in a region, it will tend to diversify programming for economic reasons. Consider: If six companies own six stations in a small market, all six will tend to gun for the highest ratings possible and put the other stations out of business. Such a strategy will almost always result in duplication of formats. . . . But when a single owner controls all six stations, there is no incentive to put the other stations out of business. He's more likely to diversify his programming portfolio to reach the largest aggregate listenership."[4]

there is a demand, the free market will meet it, and it is meeting it."[5]

President Bill Clinton saw potential benefits when he signed the Telecommunications Act of 1996 into law. The act eliminated national station ownership limits and raised local limits from four to eight stations. Clinton explained his decision after signing the bill. He believed the act would promote investment and competition. He also thought the measure would have benefits for citizens. It would help them gain access to more information, improve the quality of service, and give them more control over what kinds

Minority Voices

Free Press is an organization focused on reforming the media. It extends the concern beyond political and social balance to racial balance. Free Press argues that the U.S. media lacks diversity when its ownership and staff members consist of too many white, upper-class men.

A 2007 Free Press study found that 33 percent of U.S. citizens are people of color. Only 3 percent of television station owners fit that description. Women made up 51 percent of the population but just 5 percent of television station owners. Latino-owned television stations were only available to 21 percent of Latino-American households. African-American-owned television stations were available to 8 percent of African-American homes.

A 2008 study by the American Society of Newspaper Editors put the number of minority journalists working at daily newspapers at 14 percent, the same as the previous year. While other industries were improving their diversity numbers, the media was declining in the number of nonwhite owners and remaining level in staffing.

Most Radio Stations Owned

The Project for Excellence in Journalism listed the broadcasting companies with the most radio stations owned through the end of 2007:

1. Clear Channel, 636
2. Cumulus Broadcasting, 286
3. Citadel Communications, 204
4. CBS Radio, 140
5. Entercom, 114
6. Salem Communications, 97
7. Saga Communications, 91
8. Cox Radio, 79
9. Univision, 74
10. Radio One, 53

of programs they wanted to access. In Clinton's view, the bill would result in improved quality, expanded choices, and cheaper prices. Customers still would benefit from a variety of voices.

The Telecommunications Act of 1996 had immediate results. More than 40 percent of the nation's 10,000-plus radio stations were sold in the next two years, according to Klinenberg. This eliminated 700 individual owners.

The Future of Music Coalition is a nonprofit organization that researches how media policies affect the music industry. It found that the decrease in station owners meant a decrease in opportunities for recording artists to receive exposure on the radio:

Virtually every geographic market is dominated by four firms controlling 70 percent of market share or greater. In smaller markets, consolidation is more extreme. . . . Format consolidation leads to fewer gatekeepers. A small number of companies control what music is played on specific formats.

Coupled with a broad trend toward shorter playlists, this creates few opportunities for musicians to get on the radio. Further, overwhelming consolidation of these formats deprives citizens the opportunity to hear a wide range of music.[6]

Robert Short Jr. was an African-American radio station owner in Syracuse, New York. In the aftermath of the new act, he was forced to sell his station. He stated that he was no longer able to provide music and content diversity to listeners. Short told Klinenberg what led him to sell:

The playing field changed right beneath our feet. I was competing against some big companies before, but it was a relatively fair battle because they couldn't monopolize the whole advertising pie. Clear Channel moved in and took over seven stations, and a lot of small broadcasters sold their licenses. Clear Channel's operating costs were unbelievably low, because they moved their stations together, turned them into jukeboxes with voice-tracking technology and syndicated programs—which they also owned!—and they had one general manager oversee the whole group.[7]

While diversity on the radio has decreased, new outlets have opened up for musicians to showcase their work on the Internet. Musicians can promote themselves on their own Web sites or by posting videos on YouTube, a free public site. Listeners also gained the ability to download individual songs through services such as iTunes. These avenues allow listeners access to more songs, and musicians can avoid the upfront marketing costs of selling albums.

Cutting Costs

Journalism studies have indicated an improvement in local television news when cross-ownership of a newspaper exists. There has not been the same amount of research on what happens to newspaper coverage. Repeating newspaper content in different forms on the Internet or partner TV stations, however, decreases the number of journalists needed to get the reports to multiple markets. This could save media companies money.

Cost-cutting measures may be necessary to save some media outlets. Some people think that shared efforts could serve that purpose. Even without an increase in cross-ownership, however, influences from large media companies tend to reduce locally generated coverage. For example, local television weather forecasters are sometimes replaced by a corporately managed weather report. This person provides localized reports for many markets. Radio

Newspapers have been struggling economically in recent years, leading some to cut jobs.

disc jockeys can be replaced by formatted music programming produced in advance in a studio. Newspapers can rely on stories produced by other newspapers in their chain. They also obtain news from wire services. This cuts back on the need for local reporters.

Less competition within each market allows for media outlets to reduce local coverage without immediate serious business implications. The public service part of the industry can suffer.

"Frighteningly, our nation's newspapers and media are now mostly controlled by a small group of corporations whose only value is more wealth and unbridled control," *Seattle Times* publisher Frank Blethen said.[8]

Klinenberg cites U.S. Bureau of Labor statistics that show newspaper employment decreased from 455,700 in 1990 to 381,300 in 2003. That was before a wave of newspaper-staffing cutbacks reduced the workforce further in 2008. In *Fighting for Air*, Klinenberg wrote that the establishment of media monopolies in many markets forced out local owners and contributed to downsizing. He cited other media studies that have tracked the numbers. For example, New York City had eight major newspapers in 1940. By 1989, it had three. In 1923, approximately 40 percent of U.S. cities benefited from two or more locally owned daily newspapers. By 2000, that number had dropped to 2 percent, and chains owned the vast majority of daily newspapers. —

*Cesar Alamilla is program director of KTUV, a Spanish-language
radio station in Little Rock, Arkansas.*

National Hurricane Center Director Bill Read answers a reporter's
questions about Hurricane Gustav on September 1, 2008.

PUBLIC RESPONSIBILITY

he public responsibility of broadcasters has
been an issue for decades. Members of the
public depend on broadcasters, newspapers, and
other media outlets for information on everything
from local and national politics to crime reports.
When severe weather or another emergency occurs,

the media's role becomes even more important. Officials depend on radio and TV stations and newspapers that have Web sites to relay safety information quickly to the most people possible.

A year after it was created in 1927, the Federal Radio Commission (FRC) emphasized public interest in its policy statement. "If enacted into law, the broadcasting privilege will not be a right of selfishness," it stated. "It will rest upon an assurance of public interest to be served."[1] Since then, debate has continued over how to best serve the public interest. Many people think that as large media companies take hold, they become less able to uphold their public responsibility.

EMERGENCY NOTIFICATION

The Federal Communications Commission (FCC) fact sheet on the Emergency Alert System states the system was improved on January 1, 1997. The Emergency Alert System makes it easier for radio and television stations, some satellite companies, and other services to send and receive emergency information. Important messages are given to the public automatically, even if no employees are working.

The system is designed to work that way, but there is no guarantee. The people of Minot, North Dakota, can attest to that. The Telecommunications Act of 1996 paved the way for Clear Channel in North Dakota, a mostly rural state with a population of less than 640,000 people. Clear Channel owned 23 of the state's radio stations. That was about one-fourth the total number of stations operating in the state. Included in that figure were all six commercial stations in Minot, the fourth-largest city in the state.

Something went terribly wrong in Minot in the early morning hours of January 18, 2002. At approximately 1:00 a.m., a train crash in Minot sent a poisonous cloud from anhydrous ammonia fertilizer

The Emergency Alert System

"This is a test of the Emergency Alert System. This is only a test." These words are part of the test script heard on television and radio stations. The test script is only heard occasionally because the system's weekly test does not require a test script. Instead, the weekly test consists of an eight-second digital data signal. The signal contains the information necessary to test the Emergency Alert System. A monthly test also has a test script. The monthly test script is developed locally and usually contains information that is relevant to the local area.

Since January 1, 1997, all radio and television broadcast stations have been using these test procedures. Since December 31, 1998, cable systems that have 10,000 or more subscribers are part of the Emergency Alert System. They conduct these tests and have the capability to transmit emergency messages on all of their video channels.

floating over the city. Chaos followed. Crews rushed to the accident scene, a fire burned in the outskirts of the city, and smoke covered much of the area. This led many citizens to make phone calls to local 911 dispatchers. With calls flooding in, 911 dispatchers could not always relay instructions on how to stay safe. Instead, they told callers to turn on their radios and listen to the EAS reports there. This was how residents were supposed to find out they needed to close all windows and not attempt to drive through the cloud.

Centralized ownership allowed Clear Channel to broadcast over the air in Minot from other locations

Why Have an Emergency Alert System?

The Emergency Alert System is designed to provide the U.S. president with a means to address the nation in the event of a national emergency. Through the system, the president has access to thousands of broadcast stations, cable systems, and participating satellite programmers to transmit a message to the public. Neither the alert system nor its predecessors have ever been activated for this purpose. But beginning in 1963, the president permitted state and local emergency information to be transmitted using the system.

without local human intervention. Instead of a few staff members working at each of six stations, only one person was working in one of the company's two buildings that night. That person did not handle an Emergency Alert System (EAS) adjustment when the public needed it most. When the disaster occurred, busy phone lines and technological misunderstandings prevented the radio stations from informing listeners.

When Minot residents turned on their radios, there were no instructions. Instead, they heard prepackaged music from the usual blend of oldies, classic rock, pop, country, and other music that Clear Channel offered. One man died after breathing in the toxic cloud. More than 100 people were treated at a local hospital. More than a thousand people ended up needing medical care for health problems after the incident.

No Answer

Power surges had kept emergency officials from being able to activate the system without the help of a radio station employee. Attempts to reach the station by telephone led to frustration. Minot Police Lieutenant Fred Debowey said he rang the stations repeatedly but did not get an answer. Eventually, a former station employee assisted with getting

Some people have blamed radio giant Clear Channel for not fulfilling its public responsibility when a train derailed in Minot, North Dakota.

preliminary messages on the air two hours after the fact.

Later, Lieutenant Debowey admitted that the failure to notify citizens of the disaster was partially the fault of the emergency officials. Because of the power surge, the Minot Central Dispatch was unable to send the EAS signal. If Clear Channel had received the signal, they would have automatically sent it out on their radio stations. Furthermore, the department's second attempt at sending a signal, this time using the old Emergency Broadcasting System, also failed because the system needed routine maintenance. Some argue that the crisis in Minot could have been prevented if the EAS was working properly in the first place. Clear Channel claims that the delayed warning was a result of the EAS not being installed by the local authorities. The company asserts that their employees worked hard to assist the public during and after the crisis.

However, some people recognize that the disaster in Minot is an example of how outside ownership can negatively affect local communities. "The old radio stations used to cover local news," Lieutenant Debowey said. "We very seldom hear local news anymore."[2]

Instead of six stations potentially competing with each other for news, Clear Channel had one full-time news reporter for all six stations. But Rick Stensby, general manager of Clear Channel's Minot stations, said such concerns are unfounded. He said the company still must service listeners to the satisfaction of advertisers. "We have to compete with television, newspapers, and billboards," Stensby said. "If we get out of whack, we would be whacked with the advertisers."[3]

Proponents of media regulation often point to what happened after the disaster in Minot as an example of why diverse media is important.

An employee inspects the press run of the Wall Street Journal. *Rupert Murdoch acquired Dow Jones, the paper's publisher, in 2007.*

AVOIDING CONFLICTS
OF INTEREST

*M*any journalists follow a code of ethics that prevents conflicts of interest. One example is the code posted on the Society of Professional Journalists Web site, which is used by thousands of news professionals. One section states,

"Journalists should be free of obligation to any interest other than the public's right to know."[1]

Many journalists do not want to stray from such ideals. But changes in the industry have made it more difficult to avoid conflicts of interest. Consolidation among media companies and changes in the types of ownership might alter priorities of media owners. Large companies have bought up family-owned and other companies with a long tradition in media. Some of the larger companies are chains with roots in the business. But the influence of shareholders in publicly traded companies can affect company practices. While news professionals might feel strongly about avoiding conflicts of interest, they might find themselves working for those who do not share that attitude.

Big Business

Businesses do not exist to lose money. But those managed by traditional journalists had a tendency to be less driven by the need to meet financial goals such as quarterly revenue projections. Strong community-minded journalism ideals and highly profitable business plans do not always share the same path.

In theory, purchases by large companies can provide long-term security for a media outlet by backing it with more wealth. University of Pennsylvania Professor C. Edwin Baker is the author of *Media Concentration: Why Ownership Matters.* He told a 2004 Senate hearing that diverse, independent local journalistic staffs help keep politicians and corporations in line. In turn, this benefits the public. Baker wrote an opinion article on the subject for the *Seattle Times*. The piece explained why he believes a greater number of owners involved in the media serves the public interest by reducing the potential for conflicts of interest:

Media mergers put papers and broad- casters into the

Code of Ethics

The Society of Professional Journalists publishes its Code of Ethics on its Web site. The Code of Ethics begins with the following preamble:

Members of the Society of Professional Journalists believe that public enlighten- ment is the forerunner of justice and the foundation of democracy. The duty of the journalist is to further those ends by seeking truth and providing a fair and comprehensive account of events and issues. Conscientious journalists from all media and specialties strive to serve the public with thoroughness and honesty. Professional integrity is the cornerstone of a journalist's credibility. Members of the Society share a dedication to ethical behavior and adopt this code to declare the Society's principles and standards of practice.[2]

hands of executives whose career advancement depends on maximizing profits. Mergers require owners to squeeze out more profits to pay off debts created by the high bids made to secure the purchase. As too many recent examples show, the most consistent method to reduce expenses is to fire journalists. Smaller owners, free from the financial burden of paying for mergers, have more room to maintain a commitment to quality.[3]

Singular Objective

Walt Disney is one of the world's largest and most well-known media companies. Michael Eisner, who served as chief executive officer from 1984 to 2005, made his goals for the company clear in an internal memo, which read: "We have no obligation to make history. We have no obligation to make art. We have no obligation to make a statement. To make money is our only objective."[4]

Author Ben H. Bagdikian points out other concerns about the new look of media ownership. With large corporations in ownership positions, board members of large media companies are more likely to also be on the board of directors at other powerful companies. There is a lack of evidence that a conflict of interest affects decision making. Still, the appearance of conflict remains. In *The Media Monopoly*, Bagdikian writes about the problems he sees with media giants:

The gravest loss is in the self-serving censorship of political and social ideas, in news, magazine articles, books, broadcasting, and movies. Some intervention by owners is direct and blunt.

Editors have a discussion in the Newsday *newsroom after Cablevision Systems Corporation announced it had acquired the publication from the Tribune Company in 2008.*

But most of the screening is subtle, some not even occurring at a conscious level, as when subordinates learn by habit to conform to owners' ideas. But subtle or not, the ultimate result is distorted reality and impoverished ideas.[5]

Not every writer sees the issue the same way. Jack Shafer is an editor for *Slate*, a daily Web magazine owned by the Washington Post Company. Shafer argued that larger media companies have an advantage when taking a strong stand in important public debates. "Small, independently owned papers routinely pull punches when covering local car dealers, real estate, and industry," Shafer said. "Whatever its shortcomings—and they are many—only big media possesses the means to consistently hold big business and big government accountable."[6]

However, media corporations might ignore some controversial social issues that do not impact them. This is a concern of Wayne LaPierre, executive vice president of the National Rifle Association. "Minority or unpopular causes—think of women's suffrage in 1914 or civil rights in 1954—would be downplayed or dismissed to keep viewers watching and advertisers buying," LaPierre said. "That's no way to run a democracy."[7]

POLITICAL POWER

The potential for abuse was evident in Italy when media businessman Silvio Berlusconi became prime minister. Berlusconi required reporters on state television stations to follow a formula known as "the sandwich" on political stories. The government's position had to be stated first. Then, the opposing viewpoint was summarized. Each report ended with a repeat of the government's arguments. Berlusconi and his government received more than twice as much airtime on the newscasts than opponents.

In the *Columbia Journalism Review,* Alexander Stille reported that this approach was quite effective for Berlusconi. Researchers found that the television stations a person watched and for how long had more to do with who they voted for than their social class or church affiliation. The more a person watched television, the more likely he or she was to vote for Berlusconi. People who watched the stations he owned also supported Berlusconi.

Laws in the United States are designed to prevent such influence on the political scene, particularly as it applies to elections. The Equal Time Rule requires stations to make available the same amount of time on the air during election season for competing major candidates. This includes free time and paid time for advertising. Stations also must offer the same price for advertising. News coverage and other exemptions exist, but the intent is to keep access equal for national and major state-level races. The Federal Communications Commission is responsible for enforcing the Equal Time Rule.

*Italian Prime Minister Silvio Berlusconi answers reporters'
questions during a press conference.*

National Hockey League fans have complained about the coverage of hockey since ESPN no longer holds broadcast rights.

MEDIA AND SPORTS

roadcast stations often pay rights fees to sports leagues or organizations to carry events. When this happens, the stations and organizations become partners in a sense. Both entities benefit when the league, team, or athlete does well. Ratings increase, advertising rights go up, and they both make more money.

Game coverage also has a news component to it. The same broadcasters often have news programs that clearly require journalistic standards in coverage. These journalists work with the same ethical codes as others in the profession. But despite their best efforts, the relationship between sports and media often creates conflicts of interest.

Consumer Complaints

Le Anne Schreiber is a former *New York Times* sports editor who serves as ombudsman for ESPN. ESPN bills itself as "The Worldwide Leader in Sports." As ombudsman, Schreiber serves as the public's representative to ESPN. She evaluates concerns expressed by the public and looks for ways the company can improve. In 2007, viewers and listeners raised questions about the role of rights-fee agreements in ESPN's news coverage and commentary. Schreiber addressed their concerns:

Imagine the New York Times owning half of the Broadway theaters whose plays it reviews. Or imagine CNN paying billions of dollars for exclusive multiyear rights to cover the war in Iraq. Imagine the temptation to recoup investment by piquing advance interest and prolonging the runs of plays and wars.

That kind of temptation, almost inconceivable for other news organizations, is a chronic circumstance of journalistic life at ESPN, and has been since the day it first paid good money to televise an event while also covering it as news.[1]

Schreiber listed some of the common complaints that she has received. For example, hockey fans think their sport gets less attention from ESPN now that the network no longer has rights to televise National Hockey League games. Sports fans who do not follow NASCAR think the auto-racing series gets more attention now that ESPN televises races. Football receives year-round coverage on ESPN. The network now carries Monday Night Football games from the National Football League and has an ownership interest in the far-less-established Arena Football League.

"There is this notion that we drive a sport's popularity. I may be naïve, but I think we reflect it."[2]

—Craig Lazarus,
ESPN vice president of
studio productions

Some viewers have raised questions about how rights-fee agreements have affected coverage on ESPN.

At times, sports organizations have even influenced staffing decisions. The Masters, one of golf's four major championships, pressured CBS into removing Gary McCord as an announcer in the annual event in 1994. Tournament officials disapproved of some of the analogies McCord used to describe the course, Augusta National. Frank DeFord, a highly respected *Sports Illustrated* writer and National Public Radio commentator, talked about the effects of such actions:

Everybody is somehow silenced by these contracts and the fact that too many networks are chasing too few properties. You don't want them coming to you and saying, "You had these rotten things to say about us three years ago." Everything is inhibited by the fear of losing these contracts. So everything is played down the middle of the fairway, every time.[3]

NHL versus AFL

ESPN Ombudsman Le Anne Schreiber said disappointed National Hockey League fans frequently compare the treatment of hockey to coverage received by the Arena Football League when complaining to the network. ESPN's research showed that the National Hockey League suffered a 28 percent decline in airtime on 1:00 a.m. *SportsCenter* shows between March 2004 and March 2007. These shows feature the most live highlights on the network. The league had a broadcast contract with ESPN in 2004 but not in 2007. New segments taking up time on *SportsCenter* accounted for some of the drop. Low ratings when games were televised also could have contributed to the impression of producers that the public was less interested in the league.

The Arena Football League receives similar low ratings on live game broadcasts. The league shifted rights to show many of its games on ESPN when the network became a 10 percent owner in the league. The Arena Football League's airtime on *SportsCenter* was not tracked to provide a comparison to National Hockey League coverage. However, ESPN Executive Vice President for Content John Skipper acknowledged that "we will help grow the league across all of our multimedia platforms."[4]

PARTNERSHIPS

The connection between media outlets and the events their employees cover are not isolated to broadcast-rights fees. Some media organizations own teams. Many pay to advertise in stadiums. Some even pay the larger fees necessary to have naming rights on stadiums or as corporate sponsors of events.

The Tribune Company, which publishes the *Chicago Tribune*, owns the Chicago Cubs. As of 2008, the Tribune Company was trying to sell the team. In the meantime, the relationship has caused some people to be concerned. Chicago mayor Richard M. Daley is a fan of the city's other major league team, the White Sox. He thought the two teams did not receive fair coverage. "How can you compete with . . . Tribune?" Daley said. "I mean give me a break. They own the Cubs, they own WGN Radio, TV, and CLTV. You think you are going to get any publicity for the White Sox? You can't. Let's be realistic."[5]

NBC partnered with the World Wrestling Foundation in 2001 to create the XFL. The professional football league lasted for just one season because of low television ratings. Free-market advocates would argue that despite the XFL's media ties, it failed because consumers did not find it entertaining. The free market still decided what would be broadcast.

Rivals

While rights fees can make media companies and sports entities into partners in some endeavors, they are becoming opponents in others. The development of the Internet has increased the ways in which teams, leagues, and league-partnered Web sites distribute information about their leagues. Leagues now run or have direct connections to Web sites with recognizable names such as NFL.com, MLB.com, NBA.com, and NHL.com. Fans can visit these sites to read coverage of the sport. In many ways, the coverage on these Web sites resembles information formerly found only through newspapers and other media.

Media companies enter negotiations that go far beyond the fees paid to be the licensed broadcaster of a live event. Production of the league Web sites can be done in partnership with a media outlet. For example, the National Football League has had negotiations that could put the NFL Network in the hands of ESPN. Under such arrangements, the lines of what is media and what is promotion become even less clear. ⌐

The Tribune Company, publisher of the Chicago Tribune, owned the Chicago Cubs. This led to concerns about fair coverage.

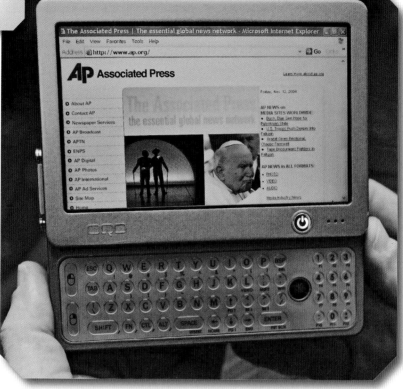

A journalist views the Associated Press Web site
on a wireless personal computer.

THE INTERNET ERA

he Internet has been a useful research
tool since late in the twentieth century.
Those who have an Internet connection can obtain
information almost instantly on a historical event,
a news story, or other subject of interest. With the

click of a button, a search engine provides a long list of potential resources.

Those who support changes to the cross-ownership rules often point to the diversity available on the Internet. In addition to traditional media outlets, bloggers and citizen journalists have started using the Web to reach an audience. With so many voices just a click away, some say the concentration of local media ownership does not matter as much.

Quantity or Quality?

While the Internet contains a large quantity of information, the quality has been debated. Some people argue that the Internet merely gives people access to similar information that is repeated in a large number of sources. While the list of search results might look long, the actual information contained in those sources is not always varied.

Changing World

A 2007 news release from the Federal Communications Commission explained how the Internet had changed the need for media cross-ownership rules: "The media marketplace has changed considerably since the newspaper/broadcast cross ownership was put in place more than thirty years ago. Back then, cable was a nascent service, satellite television did not exist and there was no Internet. Consumers have benefited from the explosion of new sources of news and information. But according to almost every measure newspapers are struggling. At least 300 daily papers have stopped publishing over the past thirty years. Their circulation is down, their advertising revenue is shrinking and their stock prices are falling. Permitting cross-ownership can preserve the viability of newspapers by allowing them to share their operational costs across multiple media platforms."[1]

Much Web content is a repeat of information produced by a newspaper or wire service. News videos often come from the same material that is available on television. The same can be true of sound recordings from radio.

In its 2005 State of the News Media report, the Project for Excellence in Journalism concluded that the use of the Internet by large organizations is disappointing:

> If the innovative edge for online media is to come from great media institutions with their resources and experience, the signs so far are disappointing. The content they offer on the Web, while improving in volume, timeliness, and technological

Blogging and Reporting

Bloggers, a term used for the writers of Web logs or "blogs," generally comment on material reported on by other sources. The blogs that become most famous, however, are often those that include original reporting and insight from an expert with connections to an area of interest.

The George Polk Award is given out by Long Island University for excellence in legal reporting. It was awarded to a blogger for the first time in 2008. The award recognized Joshua Micah Marshall of the Talking Points Memo Web site. Marshall, a columnist and former magazine editor, uses his blog to address many political issues. Although Marshall's blog clearly takes a partisan approach, he combined it with reporting that received attention and led to the award.

Marshall broke many of the details on the story when the George W. Bush administration was tied to the firing of U.S. attorneys whom it considered to be disloyal to the White House. When details were revealed, Attorney General Alberto Gonzalez ultimately resigned.

sophistication, remains still significantly a morgue for wire copy, second-hand material, and recycled stories from the morning paper.[2]

Stories originally reported on and written by newspaper reporters can take on a different form in other media. "Newspapers provide the core editorial content for radio, television, and Internet news sites, from those produced by major media companies to those made by solitary bloggers," Eric Klinenberg wrote in *Fighting for Air*. "Without newspaper reporting, most other news media would have little basis for their journalism."[3]

ADVANTAGES AND DISADVANTAGES

An advantage for consumers is that on many sites the news is available long before a morning newspaper arrives. The Internet also does not have the same space constraints as other media forms, so more of the day's news is within reach. Newspaper editors and network news producers often leave some stories uncovered because they do not all fit in the number of pages or time allotted.

Each news organization now has gained the potential to reach a wider audience through the

Internet. Readers on the East Coast, for example, can instantly gain access to newspaper or television stories from the West Coast. This would have taken significant effort in the past.

However, some have argued that cross-ownership rules still are necessary to protect local news outlets. Gene Kimmelman, vice president for federal and international affairs for the Consumers Union, made this argument in a 2007 interview on PBS:

> On the Internet, you get your newspaper, dot-com, you get your broadcast station, dot-com. It's the same sources of news using new media, new technology. . . . So we're worried about too few owners controlling the points of view, the bias, the information presented in local news, and all the new media being furthering and amplifying those voices, rather than providing diversity and competition. . . . Yes, all around the world you get more information. You can get news from Africa and Asia. But if you wanted it about your local community, it's your local newspaper and your local broadcasters you need to turn to for that reporting.[4]

Political blogger Michael Brodkorb covered the 2008 U.S. Senate race between Norm Coleman and Al Franken.

Mel Karmazin, former president and chief executive officer of Viacom, testified in 2003 before the Senate Commerce Committee.

THE FUTURE

efore, during, and after the changes created by the Telecommunications Act of 1996, debate has continued with intensity. There remain strong proponents of further deregulation of the media business. They argue that it is a necessity for the survival of established media outlets and the development of new ones in a changing world. Those on the other side of the debate are no less vocal about their concerns.

Randolph May points to all the media options—large and small—that exist. With all of these options, he thinks it is no longer necessary for government to concern itself with who owns what. May is a senior fellow at the Progress & Freedom Foundation, a Washington DC organization that supports loosening of media ownership. He stated that a lot of consolidation would have to take place before legitimate antitrust concerns arose. The number of Web sites and cable television stations has increased options for consumers. "Now that we have all this media, we're in a position where we don't need to have the government dictate who can own media outlets," May said.[1]

The media's role in protecting democracy is frequently noted by those who would like to stop the momentum of consolidation. "For the media to have a single-minded emphasis on the bottom line is dangerous for democracy," according to author and University of Pennsylvania law professor C. Edwin Baker. "Unlike many companies whose main business is providing individual consumers with goods they value, the press provides value to the public at large."[2] Baker said a person does not have to read the newspaper or watch television to benefit from strong reporting. Everyone benefits when members of the media uncover corruption or wrongdoing. Strong investigative reporting does the public a service by discouraging such behavior. According to Baker, that is why members of the media need to continue their commitment to quality reporting and not just the bottom line.

MORE DECISION MAKERS

The decisions concern such controversial topics that they may stray beyond situations where the Federal

---

Who Owns What

As of 2008, the four largest television networks were owned by companies that have varied media interests.

CBS: Viacom owns CBS as well as 39 television stations, 184 radio stations, The Movie Channel, BET, Nickelodeon, TV Land, MTV, VH1, Simon & Schuster publishing, Scribner, and Paramount Pictures.

NBC: General Electric owns NBC. It also owns 13 television stations, CNBC, MSNBC, and Bravo.

ABC: The Walt Disney Company is ABC's corporate parent. Disney owns 10 television stations, 50 radio stations, ESPN, A&E, the History Channel, Discover magazine, Hyperion publishing, Touchstone Pictures, and Miramax Film Corp.

Fox: News Corporation owns the Fox Broadcasting Company. It also owns 26 television stations, FX, Fox News Channel, TV Guide, the Weekly Standard, New York Post, DirecTV, HarperCollins publishers, Twentieth Century Fox film production, and the Internet site MySpace.

Communications Commission (FCC) has clear
and absolute authority. Many of these decisions
may be subject to continued legislative and judicial
involvement. When the FCC decided to relax
ownership limits in 2003, its actions were intended
to be even more extreme. But the results were
reduced somewhat when Congress became involved.
Without the government review of the FCC decision,
the FCC might have completely done away with the
cross-ownership ban. Additionally, the television
station ownership limitation would have climbed to
45 percent of the national market.

In 2003, the U.S. House of Representatives
responded with a 400–21 vote in support of an
appropriations bill that would keep the television
ownership limits as they were. Supporters of the
FCC decision fought back. President George W.
Bush issued a warning that he would use his veto
power if Congress stopped the FCC decision.
Eventually, a compromise was reached. Both Viacom
and News Corporation were already beyond the
35 percent national limit and would have to sell
off stations if the old limit held up. The cross-
ownership ban was preserved for the time being.
But the national limit rose to 39 percent, protecting

Viacom and News Corporation in the process.

With the laws being altered in the approval process, new uncertainty followed the decisions of 2003. Cross-ownership situations that were allowed through waivers of the ban during the anticipated change were left in limbo while the issue continued to be debated. If a final decision is made to strictly enforce the original cross-ownership rules, more sales will be necessary. FCC Chairman Kevin J. Martin said that would be dangerous to the industry.

"Since 2003, when the courts told the commission to change its media ownership rules, the news media industry has operated in a climate of uncertainty. Many newspapers and broadcast stations are operating under waivers of the ban on cross-ownership. The FCC needs to address these issues in a coherent and consistent fashion rather than considering them case by case, making policy by waiver."[3]

—Kevin J. Martin, FCC chairman

Martin defended the FCC's actions in a *New York Times* opinion piece:

> I confess that in my public role, I feel the press is not on my side. But it is for this very reason that I believe this controversial step is worth taking. In their role as watchdog and informer of the citizenry, newspapers are crucial to our democracy.

> A colleague on the commission, Michael Copps, for whom I have the utmost respect, has argued that our very democracy is at stake in the decisions we make regarding media ownership.

FCC Chairman Kevin Martin tours the AT&T video control room in 2006 to learn about the latest communications technology.

I do not disagree. But if we believe that newspaper journalism plays a unique role in the functioning of our democracy, then we cannot turn a blind eye to the financial condition in which these companies find themselves. [4]

Adjusting to Technology

The ideological debates seem sure to continue. But new technological changes also appear likely to have some impact on the future of media ownership in the United States. If deregulation continues, big mergers could be the natural result of capitalism. However, developments in new media options on

Preparing for the Future

The colleges that train the next generation of journalists are another group that is interested in trying to assess what the future will hold. Programs are already more inclined to offer training in ways to produce multimedia features on Web sites. If the media continues to converge, increased emphasis may need to be placed on training journalists to handle a wider variety of technological issues. Colleges may determine that it makes less sense to train specialists on specific media concentrations and try to ensure a varied skill set for all.

the Web allow for the possibility of an emergence of a new breed of smaller, more independent media outlets. That possibility assumes there are people willing to enter an industry at a time when its established companies are showing signs of distress.

The startup costs of a Web site are much lower than that of newspaper and magazine publications. But easy access on the production end is not always matched on the news gathering end. A citizen press needs to develop a reputation before it acquires the status to gain the same access traditional media has worked to build.

The debate on how to handle ownership of existing media companies is likely to continue. Views on the laws that affect the future of media ownership form extreme opposites. Those strongly differing opinions make it more difficult to reach an understanding that is likely to appease both sides for the long term. —

A demonstrator marches and chants in protest of media deregulation in Los Angeles in 2003.

TIMELINE

1890	1891	1910
The Sherman Antitrust Act is passed. It restricts monopolies and actions that restrain free trade.	Wireless telegraphs are first used on ships.	The Wireless Ship Act passes. It sets rules for minimal radio operations on passenger ships.

1926	1927	1928
The National Broadcasting Company (NBC) is founded.	The Radio Act of 1927 passes, creating the Federal Radio Commission.	The Federal Radio Commission creates a policy statement to clarify its mission.

1912

The luxury passenger ship *Titanic* sinks off the coast of Newfoundland, Canada.

1912

The Radio Act of 1912 passes. It allows Congress to take control of radio frequencies.

1914

The Federal Trade Commission Act creates the Federal Trade Commission.

1934

The Communications Act of 1934 is passed, creating the Federal Communications Commission (FCC).

1948

Cable television service debuts.

1963

The Emergency Alert System is updated to include state and local information.

TIMELINE

1968	1975	1983
Canada's Parliament creates the Canadian Radio-television and Telecommunications Commission.	The FCC bans cross-ownership, preventing a newspaper from sharing ownership with a radio or television station in the same market.	The number of FCC commissioners is reduced from seven to five.

2002	2003	2004
The public responsibility of broadcasters is debated after a train derails in Minot, North Dakota.	The FCC creates new ownership limits for broadcast stations.	The Third Circuit Court of Appeals heard the case *Prometheus v. FCC* challenging the new limits.

1992	1996	1997
The Cable Act of 1992 passes to regulate the cable TV industry.	The Telecommunications Act of 1996 passes and eases restrictions on media ownership.	The FCC updates the Emergency Alert System to automatically send out alerts.

2006	2007	2008
The FCC seeks public input on how it should address newspaper/broadcast cross-ownership issues.	The FCC votes to allow cross-ownership of newspapers with broadcast stations in the same market.	The Senate votes against the FCC's rule, which would have ended the ban on cross-ownership.

Essential Facts

At Issue

Opposed to Deregulation

❖ Diverse media is vital to democracy, serving as a watchdog on government and business. Therefore, the media must be protected and regulated more than other industries.

❖ Consolidation of media companies potentially reduces the amount of local and diverse coverage available through radio, television, and newspapers.

❖ Beginning with the Telecommunications Act of 1996, a select group of large companies has gained too much control of the nation's media.

In Favor of Deregulation

❖ With the newspaper industry suffering through extreme financial struggles, limitations on cross-ownership between newspapers and broadcast outlets need to be removed.

❖ Free markets allow businesses and entire industries to regulate themselves through competition.

❖ Deregulation can allow supply and demand to determine the way a market operates and, in turn, influence costs.

❖ The emergence of the Internet has changed the way the public receives information, rendering some previous media laws irrelevant.

Critical Dates

April 14, 1912
The *Titanic* sank in the North Atlantic. A radio distress signal that was missed by two nearby ships and the death of approximately 1,500 passengers contributed to the passage of the Radio Act of 1912.

1934
The Communications Act of 1934 was passed and the Federal Communications Commission (FCC) was created.

1975
The FCC banned cross-ownership of newspapers and either a radio or television station in the same market.

1996
The Telecommunications Act of 1996 passed. This was the beginning of a series of steps that eased restrictions on media ownership.

2007–2008
The FCC voted to allow cross-ownership of newspapers with broadcast stations in the same market. The Senate voted against the FCC's rule.

QUOTES

"If we don't act to improve the health of the newspaper industry, we will see newspapers wither and die. Without newspapers, we would be less informed about our communities and have fewer outlets for the expression of independent thinking and diversity of viewpoints. The challenge is to restore the viability of newspapers while preserving the core values of a diversity of voices and a commitment to localism in the media marketplace."—*Kevin J. Martin, Chairman, Federal Communications Commission*

"We already have too much concentration in the media. Diverse, independent, and local media sources are essential to ensuring that the public has access to a variety of information."—*Byron Dorgan, Senator*

ADDITIONAL RESOURCES

SELECT BIBLIOGRAPHY

"Diversity, Democracy and Access: Is Media Concentration a Crisis?" *Media Channel*. <http://www.mediachannel.org/ownership/front.shtml>.

Klinenberg, Eric. *Fighting for Air: The Battle for Control of America's Media*. New York: Metropolitan Books, 2007.

Krasnow, Erwin. "The Public Interest Standard: The Elusive Search for the Holy Grail." *CyberCemetery*. 22 October 1997. <http://govinfo.library.unt.edu/piac/octmtg/Krasnow.htm>.

"The State of the News Media 2008: An Annual Report on American Journalism." *Project for Excellence in Journalism*. <http://www.stateofthemedia.org>.

FURTHER READING

Baker, C. Edwin. *Media Concentration and Democracy: Why Ownership Matters*. Cambridge, UK: Cambridge University Press, 2006.

Einstein, Mara. *Media Diversity: Economics, Ownership, and the FCC*. Mahwah, NJ: Lawrence Erlbaum Associates, 2004.

Freedman, Des. *The Politics of Media Policy*. Hoboken, NJ: John Wiley & Sons, 2008.

Ruschmann, Paul. *Media Bias*. New York: Chelsea House Publishers, 2006.

WEB LINKS

To learn more about media ownership, visit ABDO Publishing Company online at **www.abdopublishing.com**. Web sites about media ownership are featured on our Book Links page. These links are routinely monitored and updated to provide the most current information possible.

For More Information

For more information on this subject, contact or visit the following organizations.

Federal Communications Commission
445 12th Street SW, Washington DC 20554
888-225-5322
www.fcc.gov
The Federal Communications Commission is the government agency that regulates communications by radio, television, wire, satellite, and cable.

Project for Excellence in Journalism
1615 L Street NW 700, Washington DC 20036
202-419-3650
www.journalism.org
The Project for Excellence in Journalism is a research organization that studies the performance of the media. It publishes an annual report, The State of the News Media.

Society of Professional Journalists
Eugene S. Pulliam National Journalism Center
3909 N. Meridian St., Indianapolis, IN 46208
317-927-8000
www.spj.org
The Society of Professional Journalists is dedicated to encouraging the free flow of information and promoting ethical standards in journalism.

GLOSSARY

blogs
> Web logs in which a writer shares personal views, observations, and links to other Web sites.

broadcast
> To make public by transmission through radio or television.

censorship
> The act of preventing people from reading or seeing something thought to be wrong or offensive.

chain
> A group of enterprises, such as newspapers, under one ownership.

consolidation
> The combining of smaller entities into larger groups.

contentious
> Likely to cause quarrels or disputes.

cross-ownership
> Single ownership of two or more related businesses that allows the owner to control competition.

diversity
> The inclusion of a variety of different views or people.

genre
> A category of artistic, musical, or literary composition.

grandfather
> To permit to continue based on conditions that existed before a new rule or law was passed.

indecency
> Something that is improper or offensive.

journalism
> The collection and presentation of news through the media.

media
> Agencies of mass communication.

merger
> The combination of two or more organizations or businesses.

monopoly
> The complete control of something, especially a service or the supply of a product.

network
> A radio or television company that produces shows to air over a group of stations.

new media
> The use of computers to distribute information, such as through Web sites.

ombudsman
> A person whose job is to investigate reported complaints.

regulation
> A rule issued by a government agency and having the force of law.

shareholder
> Someone who holds part ownership in a company.

superstation
> A large television station, licensed to be broadcast in multiple markets.

telegraph
> Equipment used to communicate over distance by coded signals.

veto
> To refuse to approve a new rule or law.

waiver
> The act of giving up something by choice, such as when a government agency chooses not to enforce a rule.

Source Notes

Chapter 1. Media Consolidation

1. Kevin J. Martin. "The Daily Show." *New York Times*. 13 Nov. 2007. 30 May 2008 <http://hraunfoss.fcc.gov/edocs_public/attachmatch/DOC-278113A1.pdf>.
2. "Michael Powell." *NewsHour with Jim Lehrer*. 2 June 2003. 30 May 2008 <http://www.pbs.org/newshour/bb/media/jan-june03/powell_6-2.html>.
3. Ibid.
4. Ibid.
5. Eric Klinenberg. *Fighting for Air: The Battle for Control of America's Media*. New York: Metropolitan Books, 2007. 130.
6. Jeffrey Milyo. "The Effects of Cross-ownership on the Local Content and Political Slant of Local Television News." Federal Communications Commission. Sept. 2007. 30 May 2008 <http://hraunfoss.fcc.gov/edocs_public/attachmatch/DA-07-3470A7.pdf>.
7. Katherine Skiba. "Senate Opposes Media Ownership Rule." *U.S. News and World Report*. 16 May 2008. 30 May 2008 <http://www.usnews.com/articles/news/politics/2008/05/16/senate-opposes-media-ownership-rule.html>.
8. "Statement by FCC Commissioner Michael J. Copps on Senate Vote to Overturn FCC's Flawed Media Ownership Decision." Federal Communications Commission. 16 May 2008. 30 May 2008 <http://hraunfoss.fcc.gov/edocs_public/attachmatch/DOC-282239A1.pdf>.

Chapter 2. Communications Law

1. "Susan Douglas on: The Importance of Wireless." PBS. 6 July 2008 <http://www.pbs.org/wgbh/amex/rescue/filmmore/reference/interview/douglas09.html>.
2. The Radio Act of 1927. Pub. L. 632. 23 Feb. 1927. 12 Aug. 2008 <http://showcase.netins.net/web/akline/pdf/1927act.pdf>.
3. Herbert Hoover. *The Memoirs of Herbert Hoover: The Cabinet and the Presidency, 1920–1933*. Vol. 2. New York: Macmillan, 1952. 144.

Chapter 3. The Federal Communications Commission

1. "Telecommunications History." TelecomSpace. 6 July 2008 <http://www.telecomspace.com/telecoms-history.html>.

2. Eric Klinenberg. *Fighting for Air: The Battle for Control of America's Media*. New York: Metropolitan Books, 2007. 226.

3. Ibid.

4. Ibid.

5. Anthony DeBarros. "Consolidation Changes Face of Radio." *USA Today*. 17 July 1988. 1–2.

Chapter 4. Other Countries

1. Michael McEwen. "A Report to the CRTC: Media Ownership; Rules Regulations and Practices in Selected Countries and Their Potential Relevance to Canada." Canadian Radio-television and Telecommunications Commission. July 2007. 7 July 2008 <http://www.crtc.gc.ca/eng/publications/reports/mcewen07.htm>.

2. Ibid.

3. Ibid.

4. Ibid.

Chapter 5. Diversification

1. Kevin J. Martin. "The Daily Show." *New York Times*. 13 Nov. 2007. 30 May 2008 <http://hraunfoss.fcc.gov/edocs_public/attachmatch/DOC-278113A1.pdf>.

2. Eric Klinenberg. *Fighting for Air: The Battle for Control of America's Media*. New York: Metropolitan Books, 2007. 62.

3. William Safire. "On Media Giantism." *New York Times*. 20 Jan. 2003. 12 July 2008 <http://query.nytimes.com/gst/fullpage.html?res=9C0DE7D61530F933A15752C0A9659C8B63>.

4. Jack Shafer. "What Really Happened in Minot, N.D.?" *Slate*. 10 Jan. 2007. 11 Aug. 2008 <http://www.slate.com/id/2157395>.

5. Joelle Tessler. "Diversity Debate Shapes Media Ownership Rules." *CQ Weekly*. 7 Jan. 2007. 11 Aug. 2008 <http://www.mediaaccess.org/news/2007%20News/0129%20CQWeekly.pdf>.

6. Kristin Thomas and Peter DiCola. "Radio Deregulation: Has It Served Citizens and Musicians?" *Future of Music Coalition*. 18 Nov. 2002. 8 July 2008 <http://www.futureofmusic.org/research/radiostudyexecsum.cfm>.

7. Eric Klinenberg. *Fighting for Air: The Battle for Control of America's Media*. New York: Metropolitan Books, 2007. 59–60.

8. Ibid. 117.

SOURCE NOTES CONTINUED

Chapter 6. Public Responsibility

1. Erwin Krasnow. "The Public Interest Standard: The Elusive Search for the Holy Grail." 22 Oct. 1997. *CyberCemetery*. 7 July 2008 <http://govinfo.library.unt.edu/piac/octmtg/Krasnow.htm>.
2. Jennifer B. Lee. "On Minot, N.D., Radio, A Single Corporate Voice." *New York Times*. 31 Mar. 2003. 13 April 2008 <http://query.nytimes.com/gst/fullpage.html?res=9C05EED61539F932A05750C0A9659C8B63>.
3. Ibid.

Chapter 7. Avoiding Conflicts of Interest

1. "Code of Ethics." *Society of Professional Journalists*. 9 July 2008 <http://www.spj.org/ethicscode.asp>.
2. Ibid.
3. C. Edwin Baker. "Dispersed Media Ownership Serves Democratic Values." *Seattle Times*. 10 Sept. 2007. 13 June 2008 <http://commerce.senate.gov/public/_files/FrankBlethenSenateHearingTestsamplingofstories.pdf>.
4. Anup Shah. "Media Conglomerates, Mergers, Concentration of Ownership." 29 Apr. 2007. 9 July 2008 <http://www.globalissues.org/HumanRights/Media/Corporations/Owners.asp>.
5. Ben H. Bagdikian. *The Media Monopoly*. Boston: Beacon Press, 2000. 45.
6. Dan Kennedy. "Monopoly Money." *Boston Phoenix*. 10 Jan. 2002. 13 July 2008 <http://thebostonphoenix.com/boston/news_features/top/features/documents/02105018.htm>.
7. "Background on FCC Rules: FCC Opponents Speak Out." *HearUsNow.org*. 10 July 2008 <http://www.hearusnow.org/mediaownership/17/fccopponentsspeakout/>.
8. Alexander Stille. "Silvio's Shadow." *Columbia Journalism Review*. Sept./Oct. 2006. 13 July 2008 <http://cjrarchives.org/issues/2006/5/Stille.asp>.

Chapter 8. Media and Sports

1. LeAnne Schreiber. "At ESPN, Conflict of Interest Is Business as Usual." 11 May 2007. 10 July 2008 <http://sports.espn.go.com/espn/columns/story?columnist=schreiber_leanne&id=2866241>.
2. Ibid.

3. Lawrence Strauss. "Does Money Tilt the Playing Field?" *Columbia Journalism Review*. Sept./Oct. 1998. 10 July 2008 <http://backissues .cjrarchives.org/year/98/5/sports.asp>.
4. LeAnne Schreiber. "At ESPN, Conflict of Interest Is Business as Usual." 11 May 2007. 10 July 2008 <http://sports.espn.go.com/ espn/columns/story?columnist=schreiber_leanne&id=2866241>.
5. Gary Washburn. "Daley: Tribune Makes Chicago a Cubs Town." *Chicago Tribune*. 7 Oct. 2005. 6.

Chapter 9. The Internet Era
1. "Chairman Kevin J. Martin Proposes Revision to the Newspaper/ Broadcast Cross-ownership Rule." Federal Communications Commission. 13 Nov. 2007. 12 Aug. 2008 <http://www.fcc.gov/ commissioners/martin/articles/news_release_11132007.pdf>.
2. "The State of the News Media, 2005." The Project for Excellence in Journalism. 11 July 2008 <http:// www.stateofthemedia.org/2005/narrative_online_intro. asp?cat=1&media=3>.
3. Eric Klinenberg. *Fighting for Air: The Battle for Control of America's Media*. New York: Metropolitan Books, 2007. 113–114.
4. "FCC Weighs Changing Media 'Cross-ownership' Rules." *The Online NewsHour*. 17 Dec. 2007. 12 Aug. 2008 <http://www.pbs.org/ newshour/bb/media/july-dec07/monopolies_12-17.html>.

Chapter 10. The Future
1. Joanna Glasner. "Media More Diverse? Not Really." *Wired Magazine*. 30 May 2003. 10 July 2008 <http://www.wired.com/ techbiz/media/news/2003/05/59015>.
2. C. Edwin Baker. "Dispersed Media Ownership Serves Democratic Values." *Seattle Times*. 10 Sept. 2007. 13 June 2008 <http://commerce.senate.gov/public/_files/ FrankBlethenSenateHearingTestsamplingofstories.pdf>.
3. Kevin J. Martin. "The Daily Show." *New York Times*. 13 Nov. 2007. 30 May 2008 <http://hraunfoss.fcc.gov/edocs_public/ attachmatch/DOC-278113A1.pdf>.
4. Ibid.

INDEX

ABOUT THE AUTHOR

Tom Robinson has written 14 books for young readers while working as a freelance writer and editor. His career includes time as a newspaper sports editor and radio-show host as well as experience with television and Web sites. Robinson won an award from the Associated Press Sports Editors in 1998.

PHOTO CREDITS

Mark Lennihan/AP Images, cover; Gerald Herbert/AP Images, 6; Walt Unks/The Herald-Sun/AP Images, 13; P. Kevin Morley/ Richmond Times-Dispatch/AP Images, 17; AP Images, 18, 23, 25, 29; Harvey Georges/AP Images, 26; Ron Edmonds/AP Images, 33; Alan Porritt/AP Images, 34; Nathan Denette/AP Images, 37; Bryan Charlton/AP Images, 45; Jeffrey Sheldon/iStock Photo, 46; Keith Srakocic/AP Images, 55; Mike Wintroath/AP Images, 57; Andy Newman/AP Images, 58; Eric Gay/AP Images, 63; Robert Petry/ Minot Daily News/AP Images, 65; Mel Evans/AP Images, 66; Julia Gaines/Newsday/AP Images, 70; Alessandra Tarantino/AP Images, 73; Gene J. Puskar/AP Images, 74; Bob Child/AP Images, 77; M. Spencer Green/AP Images, 81; Damian Dovarganes/AP Images, 82; Jim Mone/AP Images, 87; Ron Edmonds/AP Images, 88; LM Otero/AP Images, 93; Jerome T. Nakagawa/AP Images, 95